Voices Over Art

Art text documents

Holly Crawford

Lokke

New York

Several of the early texts are re-published here. They were first published in several issues of NYArts.

One was part of the Cage's Musicircus that was a project at the Melbourne International Arts Festival.

Cover photograph by Holly Crawford, 2011
www.art-poetry.info

ISBN:978-0-9852461-2-9

To George, who is in the cover image and does not want me to talk at all when he looks at art.

I like to thank everyone who allowed me stand next to them while they talked and talked. I was standing shoulder to shoulder with them at the times. Yes, I was gazing at the art, but I was listening to you and writing down what I overheard as quickly as I could. I did not use an electronic recorder. I wanted the conversations to filter through me and not be a literal transcription The fragments and the fractured comments are an important part of the project. It reflects the actual experience, meaning I have to translate and grasp what you're saying. Just as a viewer has look at the art and then think about. When that is done it becomes a personal experience. Every viewers experience is different. I decide on a space. When I arrive I hear something, something that I consider a beginning and at some point something that seems to be a natural ending. A textual object is created from all the voices that surround me as I wander through the different art space and look at the art. I did not include any comments between the public and museum guards. They were mostly questions: "Where is the bathroom?" Once someone did turn to me and ask to borrow my pen because they needed to write something down. I consider this a form of art criticism. I was trying to find out what the viewer might be thinking when in a museum or art gallery.

I did take a break for several years, but recently did one at the art fairs in NYC in 2012. I took a break because I was told that I was becoming known and I did not want the text to be contrived.

The longest one was 12 hours in Melbourne Australia. It was part of Cage's *Musicircus* that was one of the projects at the Melbourne International Arts Festival. Yes, I have done other places. I sat at a table in Times Square and tweeted what I overheard to a flat monitor in Wels, Austria as part of a project. I also once wrote down what I overheard in dressing room in stores along 5th Avenue in NYC. That text poem was printed in an issue *Van Gogh's Ear*.

In 2004 many of the ones from NYC were printed in *NY Arts* magazine as a special project of mine on art criticism, art and poetry.

–Holly Crawford August, 2012 NYC

Where shall we go?

So

Access to the media lounge
Oh no…all the way around.

Nice to see you.

Hope you have a nice visit.

What shall we do?

I should go visit a friend.

I'm going to go… this is the lady.

How are you doing?

He's been in this business for a long time.
It's right next door.

Is this the end.

We can check it out.

What?

That was yesterday.

May I introduce her to you quickly?
Saturday morning and then…
We're going out to the suburbs
There this girl…she's a nice person…we…we…they keep saying

Months from now…I could stay here a little but…that…probably
…do you mind….John was here…
20 minutes later….

I see the idea…let's take this on the road….

John saw them

They were about to walk out the door….last summer….I can't
remember
his name…really.
What's his name?
What's my name?

I saw

I saw

I get sick of that

I like

two glasses

two glasses

I was in line

high lin
so…the whole idea…but then

she was do nice

yah

he's Italian

what would you like to drink?
Gordy said he sold some work!

Sold some work!

I would like to…but …sure why not

They’re doing a show…
I didn’t see it…
Oh well. -- Armory Art Fair, 2012

Do you … … …

think you …

can

wait …

… …

… I'm

not quite getting it,

but anyway

… … …

… … …

… I

think it's

… … art

… (touch)

… there's

something …

haunting …

about

it.— ***Christo and Jeanne-Claude, The Gate, Central Park, New York*, The Metropolitan Art Museum**

(cough)
…
what
…
there's a
…
it looks like
…
they took it
…
(cough)
…
this is just too much
…
sorry
…
I know
…
nice
…
that's good
…
(laugh)
…
hmm
…
hmm
...
Scheisse
…
ya
…
ein
…
Scheisse
…
zig
…
Scheisse
…
nein
…
dede dede dede
…

who knows

…

no?

…

no.-- Dieter Roth, PS 1

This is what you see on the roof……………………………. ………………………………… Wow! Look at this! The fog great atmospherics…………… …………………..I pressed it accidentally………………….. …………………What is this suppose to be?....................... ………………….. Big smile, Big smile. …………Mike! Get off it!.......... Let's take a picture. What is it?................................ I want a family picture here. ……………..You want to take a picture? ………I didn't hear the clicking sound. You push down and then push down again……………………………………………………..He kind of balances things. Ok. -- *Andy Goldsworthy on the Roof*, The Metropolitan Museum of Art

We're moving pretty slowly ……………………………………………………………………… ………………………………………………………………….. Are we waiting? We could go and come back in 15 minutes…. Why not?............... .... ……………It's a special exhibit. …Look a legal parking space. Do you want to move the car?............... There's….. a………………… …….line…………………….. inside………………………… ……………………………. I'm waiting in line right now at the Jewish Museum. The Jewish Museum……………………………………………………………… …………………………………………………………… ……………………………………………………………………… ……………………………………………………………..Are you in line? ……………………………………………………………….This is one of his sculptures. You can see the African influence. Did he go to Africa? No……...Some of these are famous. He had…the reclining woman. Some of this stuff doesn't have his style. ……………… What number is this? It's a little confusing. Didn't Spinoza convert in the end? They're not telling saying what the reason is? Why is this painting hanging upside down?................................. She was a smart lady. She had a lot of money…………………..…. ……………………………………..I like the way he texturizes the skin. …The legs over here with the hair on them………. Do you want to see something else? *—Modigliani, Beyond the Myth*, The Jewish Museum

…..I'm sure we've been there. It seems like…but, that doesn't look like…but it could be…I like that one. …Just look at the green outside that window.   … Turn that thing off. Honey, turn it off……he was married to…………………….. ……………the American flag………………………………

—*Childe Hassam*, The Metropolitan Art Museum

…………………………………………………………………………

………………………………

……………………..(point)…

it…um…………………………

……..(whisper)………………………………………………..(wh

isper)………………………………………………………..(whisp

er, whisper) ……….(point)………. hee-hee……………………….

………………………………..

…………………………………………….do you want to….

—*Get Off: Exploring the Pleasure Principle*, The Museum of Sex

…
…
…
…
It’s
…
Spring
…
Street
…
…
…
…
Düssuldorf
…
…
ah…—*Indexing the World*, The Metropolitan Art Museum

We're on the Metro North train...that's ...

Right…………………………..

………………………………..

Shh…shh………………………………………funny………it's gorgeous…high traffic….you'd think that it would just disappear…disintegrate……………………………………..well, I guess it was designed by him…..White Plains…the carpet is the exhibition…or really….the fabric…art?...whether it's art or not I just generally like it………………………………..this is the installation….I'm walking on it?........some times they have events in the area……………………………………………27,000 square feet of carpet ……...using…..emphasizes…I don't ….what the hell is he talking about. It's carpet, broadloom carpet. Somebody got conned. Wonder what he got paid? A rose, is a rose is a rose. So this is what 27,000 square feet looks like. It looks like a 1940s living room …………………………..what is the pattern, exactly? That goes to that, that goes to that and there are strips and that goes to.....—*Rudolf Stingel, Plan B*, Grand Central Terminal-Vanderbilt Hall

there's

nothing

upstairs

—PPOW, Von Lintel Gallery, Pink Blossoms, and Gallery Henoch

touch it

(bang, bang)

I touched it

(bang)

look, look, look

(bang)

(touch)

(bang)

(lie)

(lean)…(sit)…(sit)

(bang, bang, bang, ratty tap-tap-tap)

(touch)

(climb)… (stand) … (touch)

(sit)…(photo)

(touch)

(touch)

(touch)

--Franz West, *Recent Sculpture,* Lincoln Center & Doris C. Freedman Plaza

____

____

____

____

__rooms_______

____

____ __________

____

____

______________________ _________________________ paintings

____

____

______________________imagine ____

____

control____

____________mathematical ___________________________________

____

wonderful____

____

____

____

—*Agnes Martin's Early Paintings 1957-67,* Dia:Beacon

……We could……………….. you just found the right

spots………..this could be….. ……..I love it………………..

………I am just starting to….. relax………………….there is another thing that just came to mind.

-- Lemons Contemporary

This is the summer group show of the gallery artists…
r-i-g-h-t, right, right.

--*Group Show,* Kashya Hildebrand Gallery.

Do you know what it means?
Or what he thinks about? Anything else here?
Is he an old guy?
Oh……………………………………………………
I like the middle one.
I think they should be separate paintings.
…
I guess they're things that have happened
all in the same space. *– Seismic Disturbance, Lohin Geduld Gallery.*

Hi.

…hi, ………I'm here….

You need the password?

……The password?...um…here it is…you need to say it…

.. . 'gert frobe'…

what's the password?.........

..How does this thing open?

...Do you have a butterfly knife? No..

—*Counter Culture, Flux Factory, Secret Places, 2004,* Bowery Martial Arts, New Museum.

[empty]

--*Lot-EK:Mobile Dwelling Unit,* Whitney Museum

…she died….
(SILENCE)

Did you like the show?

--Ana Mendieta: Earth Body Sculpture and Performance, 1972-1985, Whitney Museum

…that's the impression I got…in that sense…I tried to do that years ago…before the big buildings……I guess… thought this was a whole new way of looking at the world…um

--*Ed Ruscha and Photography,* Whitney Museum

collection, Los Angeles, interesting, time, words, drew, gas stations, if, I, choose, wonder, surface tension, drool, better, grapes, drool, better, water, sky and water, more sophisticated, kooks, kooks, see, think, like, love, kind of cool, end.

--*Cotton Puffs, Q-tips, Smoke and Mirrors, The Drawings of Ed Ruscha,* Whitney Museum.

There's a lot of art…

I have to see it six more times…I have to work the show…nice to meet you… right…so, you're from Ohio…I had no idea…you have the Rock 'n Roll Hall of Fame…spread the good word…it's fabulous…whose the artist?...he's speaking at the MET…what about New Year's…looks British…yes, yes…it's a new acquisition…I like this better…it's crass and sophomoric…excellent, excellent…I know, perfect…yes, yes… that reads, 'paint on wall,' look what it says 'paint on the wall'... I don't know…this is …not compared to the stuff upstairs…………………………………………………………. ……………………………………………………………………… …………I've only been in New York for six weeks…and then...did you…did you see this…they're projecting right in the room…what…let's go down a level…that's the membership that gets you in free…I don't know why I got it, honestly…most have something to do with…yes, yes…you have to schedule…the Europeans do it…did you get it…out of the blue…maybe because I've been a member for years…I go the movies…if you go nine times…I joined because of the films, not the art…where to you live?...Union Square…Hoboken…I've moved…57…I had no idea………………what this is…no wait…it's like…oh, you're kidding…she does wonderful work…she really helps her people…this space it perfect…take you camera out…exposures…three years…that's right…you're right here…what do you want to do?...I don't know…it's that or white on white…the sad thing is I was waiting for you...I'm at the eye, Magritte…where are you? I think…is Paloma a painter…on the floor…no, not yet… it's downstairs…………….. ……………………………………………………………………… ……this Friday… maybe we'll see you…we have a dinner engagement…Greg loves Klee…Brancusi…yes, Brancusi…keep going…then you reach the end…and he was starving…right…so it may be a dream…that might explain it…all these things…that have been hidden for all these years……………………………………………………………… ……………………..This room is almost exactly the same…I'm living out of boxes…I didn't know…I don't remember this, do

you?...there's some movement…you see that…who's the kid that did Mercury…that's true, so he's old school…it seems so…if you look at it…the reason…it may be original, but it was like…let me research…what's your cell number?...two Gris and three Picasso's…overwhelming…you just look at this one and then let's go…I think it shows…did you see that room?...I was just going to say…I need the ladies room……..
………………………………………………………………………
………………………giving it the once over…this makes the Whitney look like ……would you like some of these? I wonder…you're not leaving until I'm done…they like catalogue every single thing… actually I wish I could have seen it…it has steel walls…it was basically like…oh…been there…there was an internal stairs…you want to go up……………………………………………………………………
……………………………………… there is something warm about this…I want to meet…meet us on two…you can always come back…do you want to look at photography…I went on a date with her and nothing happened… that's what I said, 'we need your input… 'burn off the hairs around my nipple….' …her parents love me…all of a sudden…each and every time…as opposed to?...would you like some more wine? He tries to make it easy for me. I don't know how to make it all work… I'll do it a couple of times… I love it. It's like….It's hard…I think this is pretty cool…I don't think it sucks…I think it vastly overrated… I like it…I know…Should we get into the coat line?

-- MOMA Re-Opening, November 2004, New York

I haven't read any reviews…
you need to check that bag…
do you hear "Somewhere Over the Rainbow"
… no… no?... you don't?, I do…
I think it starts on this floor…this guy is so f...ked…where's the bathroom?

your life's a video…she gets a lot of press…cool…the artist was here yesterday…what's downstairs? I didn't like the first floor…it's raining…the layered painting…un huh...money…scary…let me just stand here…it looks like… fetish…there's an arrow… actually …what is it?...the 60s…it' the Beatles…same thing…did you ever read?…I write creative fiction…your too close…you can see a story progress…can't do that yet…why not?…do you see that?…this is getting out of control…all you need is this, then you can recreate it… the experience…thirsty?…creepy…I looked at the motorcycle and thought that would be debated...let's just walk down…that was six years ago…you know how crazy people get… I want to touch everything…I think this is really beautiful… I got out of bed this morning…let walk around it…we did…what the hell is that?...I don't think so…this was in Chelsea… do you want me to stand in line for you?…no way…excuse me…too crowded…I'm sure it's very nice inside…when you look at the work as a whole…some of it …compositionally …their kind of the same, look at the tattoos …anyway …I missed this whole section…this is the one…oh, no. not this…think it's about 2 or 3 hours…where are the restrooms…you know what it is?...I'm starving…I skipped a lot of stuff on the third floor…did you see the mirrors?...I'm glad I came… I'd been wondering, how do you get to 75th and Madison?
Let's go for a soda… a cup of coffee? a hot chocolate.

--Whitney Biennial, Wed. 3/31, Thurs. 4/8, & Friday night 4/9. 2005

How much are they? it's not like their beautiful…I would like to know, in general…170, 150, 140…what's your number…sold…ok…we're headed through…it's…that keeps it so high…that's what I mean…he had…of course…years ago…do you know what they're worth?...he has one in his basement…he won't sell…can't buy it now…I use to buy his stuff…investment…you can't…everyone…what is it going to be worth…$100,000 or less inflation, if you think about it. You stand in line. It looks like a line. Maybe it will move quickly. Oh yea… Did you just go there? Let me show you this…ok…most people are pretty punchy…Double shot of Jack Daniels…I'm trying to take it easy…what parties did you go to last night? I didn't. I just went back to the hotel. I feel asleep and when I woke up, I realized it was too late. I missed everything.

Did you go to Scope yet? No. They had a party last night. Some like it, some say it sucked. Most of the art at NADA…I didn't see anything that jumped out at me. …ok…they guy playing the guitar while standing on his head in a bucket. I wanted to punch him in the stomach. There was this naked guy. Where is he at the show?...hi, how are you? Good to see you…very busy…do you need all these chairs?...where trying to make a deal…let me talk to them…no, it's ok…I might go for the bargain basement…that's fine…it seems so…he never answers the phone…beauty is in the eye of the beholder…look…if you…did you….for…oh, I see…I don't remember her at all…now let's go…I just want to buy a cup of coffee…. Basel-Miami Art Fair 2005—Central Plaza

Deeply ashamed…yes, you…
are you having fun?
Ja…dom..merci..say bon..pe..et la de un j…Charles..ja ma…ha
ha…oui…ost…heim mesein..slu…de…le.le..a le…ha, ha, ha.ha..
see, tat no…mou
see, it's too late.
Are you joking? It's tomorrow.
Here's my card.
Av wor..bon suare…

(puff, puff)x100

Yelling, push, pow and blam!

… ah, oui

oh you found my other..

oui

da cou

no

Palais de Tokyo, Paris 2005

18:55:…

Let's play it by ear…………are you going up there…not too bad…back to her
Original place…so a soon as I think finish my dear…you do realize that…I got
Really excited…sweet…what's this about….
Fantastic…
One night…not running
Through out…this is how much
Talk about it already…

Program…
Rests over there
Is this the main area?
…..
You know….yes…and it's really…
Free….performances
So intense.

He's ever stupid to….
To find it…
Here they are…
Sorry
How are you?
I'm trying to see.
It going to be chaos…I'll come with you.
Oh, …sorry…no….
Music…
Avant-garde…in 2%...and it was this…

19:15:47

Baritone sax
The botanical garden
The saxophone
It was pretty cool.
So this …it's good
It takes away from….
Just in this whole area…there's Cage.

Where does John Cage fit into all of this?
He was a great performer, not a composer…dusk
Til dawn…it reminds me…
I like………

(Hi, I was in the limo)

19:26:15

I don't know….but
I think …people have taken…of course…

Yes, so….

Yes, that's why then got kicked out…
That idea…and Alan and I
He's into partying………how long was that
Thank you…he's underneath….I can see her…
She's always…I thought she said something….
Everything...doing…

I could have thought.
Are you still working?
Do you see each other after work?
They're all…I sort of feel…so people…
Don't mind doing it…
15 minutes…very special…it's his
Birthday, when there's nobody else around.

I was born in Philadelphia…no I live here now.
Victoria School of the Arts…you're suppose to move
around…I love this space…at the moment.

My question is ..two more …good….to put…
Your bag…up here…what?

19.40:30

Very, very, yeah,
Yea, yea…what?
She was saying….
Random,

Right , ok…

It's turned off…same as mine…it was free for me.

My mom…it was very kind of her...give…there…quiet…one spot…
No dusk til dawn…performances everywhere…

A bunch down the stairs…I don't know where that is…a lot of its acoustic…
Dusk 'til dawn…I think I'm ready…check it out…

Who wants to be in the nest photo…that looks great…
Ok…
Non-toxic…makes it stronger…the little holes…on the weekends…
Dancing around…five stops on the train…that's nice….

Alright…this show is about…and then and then….
Installation…..advertising…energy……
Bye…………..

You really have to workout to be able to do that…it was crowded…standing
For three hours….I think…yea…

19:59:07

I loved it.

I loved it…Oh dear…that was probably a chainsaw…no
A dentist drill…it reminded me of the Pompidou…don't tell
Me that they're going to run it again…that was amazing….

20:00:55

that was 10 minutes…you want to go
that was amazing…bye…I loved it…
you have to see …every third person I see…no too tall…
to passive…amazing…hello…do we have to curtsey…royal
curtsey…that's better….he works for…you've just come back…
we've just come back….look at that picture….
Shhhh…tourist

I wish I had my camera…turn around…I could
hear…crazy…they've all got...
What's your preference….let's check this out first…

20:15:14

here, yes…we've made it! ….lovely…here we go…here she is…the camera…
lollipop, lollipop…how's it going…
it's wild...
my nephew, he's so cute, he's two and a half…really….he's still….

We're doing, well…sweaty…thank you
I don't know…I don't know…there's music along there

20:21:14

she sort of does hand movements…
about and hour…a couple of guys….yeah…he's playing without seeing…my there was in a relationship…you can see…it's like…a performance…the whole space…
an installation…it happens…in reverse…has this happened before…this particular version…in the world of sound art…he collaborated with Merce Cunningham…process…
so interesting…
a bit obsessive…
look like…I don't know…
I can't see her…
Yes, it's nice…I been before…she's so…al you need…I've seen the film…
It's good…not Rocky Horror…yes, she's very funny…
I can't tell the difference…a couple of shows in the far east…yes.
I haven't seen her…I thought …sure…yeah…working overtime.
I know she's very good…she did…who's that woman…that English woman…
early 60s…she was…yea, yea…right, right…ok. Ok…more about the scene.

20:34:25

Yes, let's go see it…Wednesday night TV.

Yeah, yeah, yeah. Really? Monday night.
Absolutely…it doesn't matter. It's all over now.
I said the other day…don't worry…
The performance…

20:39:02

it's so much fun

yes

I know

I know

I have a little dance piece coming on later

20:43:15

strange…let's go over there…that's the system…first of all….

20:46:59

you have a couple of minutes before you start…do you want to jump on the stage?

From the fairest creatures we desire increase,
That thereby beauty's rose might never die,
But as the riper should by time decrease,
His tender heir might bear his memory;

But thou contracted to thine own bright eyes,
Feed'st thy light's flame with self-substantial fuel,
Making a famine where abundance lies,
Thyself they foe, to they sweet self too cruel.
Thou that art now the world's fresh ornament,
And only herald to they gaudy spring,
Within thine own churl, mak'st waste in niggarding.
Pity the world, or else this glutton be,
To eat the world's due, by the grave and thee.

(William Shakespeare, Sonnet One, read to me by David Adamson as part of his performance)

20:54:08

he goes on like this…that's it…it …you love him…tell him to meet me at the certain spot…
nice to see you....

20:59:06

And them…you wait there…
No, you wait here…

Just do it...really? really

Intriguing …yes, yes…I really wanted to do …it's full…can we go somewhere else…let's go over there…we want to walk around…I want to go home now…can we have a look around…ok, kids…let's go….how do you know James….he studies…at the moment…mostly everything….

20:06:50

At the same time….yea, it's been interesting…sounds good…everybody ready…let's do it. Popcorn on the way home…..Dave was already asleep today…

high tech version…I seen the diagram…the art pushing up against…lots of pressure…that goes down…goes up and down…increases as it goes down…let's go down

here

come down the stairs

21:17:59

I'll see you…everything…we're doing….
Problematic …relationship…
I slept with him….
Their straight shooters…

21:27:53

the ideas…
some circuses have three rings…this one has four or five…let's see what happening over there…do you really…really ..jumping inbetween…
yea, yea…there he is…I see him…he was seating next to…excellent.

21:37:15

it's fantastic
don't tell him that…

program….

Whenever I interviewed…sonic residue…wash your hands after that…it might be broadcast…see ya…this the third time…institutions…it doesn't support…
Theater…it's great…you'll never get a gig…why…why…my house…his in a really bad place…rehab…I offered to pay…it's kind of ironic…how did you like…he did something…well done…it was great….

21:44:50

there that…a couple of hours….really nice sound

21:53:59

all this stuff going on ...do you want a drink…yea…Friday…do you want to get something here? Anyway this is it. It is really annoying. He's very obnoxious…no. no. no. he's a …not daily…are you…I had a really good time…I …I got to go…I wait here for you…my friends doing a performance…where will they be…let's go down…get an idea of the space…the space works so well…he's doing a performance…what…I don't know… friend of mine…I thought…why not…that's nice.

22:02:29

It works…what going on…I'm just watching….I'll be back in an hour…doing a show…
I'll see you…next week
So
Is it possible?
Not hanging around
Ben was sort of saying…he's gone…
Over there
I missed everything…it's over there…
A barrier here…

I like the idea of getting a …no, where is he…you can go down into it…can't you
See you later, darling….

What's going on…aside from that…Hello Michele…it's a series of pieces where he walks around taking into a the phone…over here…how funny…was that…maybe there is…that's insane…so…up…very attractive…leave me alone…where are you taking me….

22:24:04

it some from….conceptual…he's had a big week…gone out very night…what…amazing number of people around…that was nice…I really think…I'd like to sit out here…lovely…supposedly no harm…let me know…she's not coming…get a haircut…there's Paul over there…it's really not a big deal….

22:33:31

Culturally…I'm excited to tell you…hi…
he invited us up for lunch…so…there are the horn players…the windows…see them…he's always…inside painting…was it…really…that awesome… I got rejected…yea…and when…I make enough money…no worries…really…I've got to get…your book.

There's a whole stage down there. You know Edward. He's seems like a nice guy….I did it….He's…where is he going to shoot it? Newcastle…How did…he used to live in America…France…people…people, let's go…where's the….it's around… what else…I had another question.

Your success story…what happened? That's amazing. One moment. That's good. I can't believe you haven't taken that off…Lucy, is she …I meet her…really…enjoy…I thought that….

22:45:44

the blind people
can you see

this

many people
good luck

these little bits
really

the table

it's a man rattling a box
do like it
put s smile on your face
it's accessible it you don't want to be here
LEAVE
Except for Allison
She's obsessed
Huh?
This is better than football.

22:52:35

300,000

23:04:42

Excuse me.

23:08:07

Oh, I'm good.
Thank you.
Oh, inside, almost.
I think I'm out.
Cheers
See ya—
I was really beautiful…don't go…so what are you guys doing?

23:16:28

So we're…so we're…so we're…for an hour…it's been great…I know…some are…silence….high five…guest…good music….composers…musicians…yes, yip…so we've had it's great…music…place of understanding…too dedicated…jazz programs…broadcast…they don't have an understanding exactly…jazz…yes…more jazz…so hardcore…I want…program…nice to have meet you…downsize…open days… the board said you have so much capital…there is a position…it's…he won't stop….he's up 48 points…Adam Simmons is his name…fabulous…I know Albert…my girl goes to…what…yip…that get…the audience too…sounds like they've done very well…I've bee here since the start…what time is it now? …interaction…nice to have…we're going over there….

23:25:27

I thought they were building a web? …that's abstract…I was just trying to email you…Cage would be happy…one of the most amazing minds…coming up with the entire score…suggestive…I imagine…I cut my hair…It look…are you serious…change…you don't understand…like everybody they're either performing or having a look…It was a change…it's all about…ok, go.

23:35:12

Sound like birds…don't steal the balloon…bang…going this way? We're going that way. Who knows?

I actually walked up to someone whom I thought I knew I worked with…it wasn't …are we going in…see you then…nice to see you…see you later….

23:44:13

Let's see what happens first. OK

23:48:50

23:55:35

I love it.

It's not visual.

One hour.

What is that?

They performed that….

They have two more minutes….

I see….

Pizza. That looks yummy. I was in Europe. This is better than Italy. They have the worst pizza in Italy. …I believe…six years ago…the best pizza….we went there…the pizza came in two minutes…she said…she's English…yea, yea, …yea…the Yankee lady.

I saw the list

Where is she?

Walking.

My dance teacher. From university. She's coming.
She's academic…
research…
Australian dogs!
No, DANCE!
I sent her an email.

He's left brain. He's always thinking.
The right side…the left side paralyzed. Can't speak…
Doesn't show much emotion…simple…

Sticky

Shower

I ask him

Really sexy

Metaphor sex

Mental desire

We laugh

It's important.

He doesn't want to…

He doesn't want…

My grandmother…

My grandmother…

Do you.....

0:22:35

It's…
There he is…left a message on my phone…bring science into it…directly injecting the sound…human jealousy….he doesn't like it…you take it outside…you get into trouble…by whom…let's go.

0:35:49

did you see that one…we just meet… lunch? I don't think he'll ask me…I don't want to…goof…shut up…please open the door to that lift please…so there….

Oh I don't want to know about it.

I'm no fucking hippy.

What do you call a fish with no eyes?

Went down the road some way….

1:12:28

How does every single…hello…obviously…must be chemistry….yes, obviously…gay…nothing…
It's very important. Let find James. I stopped drinking. Can you image….more famous…we don't…glow….

1:24:48

We'll come back at 5.

I was blinded by the light.

Exactly.

What does the beauty of heaven have to do with us?

I was wondering.

What do you do?

Occasionally you can hear a phrase.

I've been just roaming.

I can't see, here.

See you soon.

Bye.

She at the piano.

She's …this is …experience…it's…

1:34:--

it's really quiet

you're sort of really committed after this

there is no responsibility to stay

that's true

that's true

do you have a lighter?

you better not move

fucking assumptions

are you going to be around?

please do

would you like one? it smells great

George

Ray

He brought his guitar and amp.

The challenge is to stand there….

Some hot girl

just myself

the spider…

1:53:25

1:58:59

I gave it to a small child…then she walked past…I gave it to her….

Where did you get the print out?

They may still be there.

We sold out.

It's been a balloony night.

I think some where signed.

He was very exhibitionist. Dancing, singing…good space…it's been open for five years…very cool….

strange…I remember when I was 18….he knew…you were about to run away…otherwise…I think I know who he was…he had a discussion…fish tank…early 70s…taking so many drugs…proved two things…that's right…he had a big fish at the library…they wouldn't let him borrow enough books…he was always dressed in a blue blazer…he's a stuck PhD. he never left campus…he's homeless now…he lives on campus…there are plenty of places to get inside and hide…security…what are they going to do?...drinking policy now…three standard drinks for women…five for men…that's university policy now… really need to go to the bathroom.

2:12:22

She's from the library …came to our meeting…it's just…I don't understand…I wondered what happened to you…she'll turn up…somewhere.

2:40:57

2:58:27

musicians

dynamic

bye

bye

see this guy

too easy

yea

what do you do

sweet

well ok

all crazy

tomorrow night the party

you know how these things are

I don’t know the schedule

Ok

Cool

So you do a show

He’s a gentleman

I saw him a couple of days ago

I emailed him jus to say “hi”

Meet me at the café

He’s very, very

Oh.

3:13:02

he's like

he's very jealous

it's late

Know I don't

Bye

I live here

He seems pretty young

He's a teacher

The other guy

So much shit

Fucking asshole

I everyone I know here

The whole culture

The high school culture

It's very much

We'll you please sit down…I can't see

I went to a school…there were no…but

3:24:53

it's just that whole scene

Melbourne International Arts Festival

The next one…everyone….

3:33:56

Is there anyone around to watch it?

3:38:07

Is there a bar?

A drink?

No

Performances

Fuck them.

3:40:07

my aunt

she was

3:40:49

3:46:18

now we get it

no

yah

no

yah

3:57:55

my place

4:00:12

I heard something

4:06:51

4:18:--

4:23:--

4:27:--

4:33:09

It’s the birth of an idea

4:34:--

sonnet 153
the last one

The little Love-god lying once asleep
Laid by his side his heart-inflaming brand,
Whilst many nymphs that vowed chaste life to keep
Came tripping by, but in her maiden hand
The fairest votary took up that fire,
Which many legions true hearts and warmed;
And so the general of hot desire
Was sleeping, by a virgin hand disarmed.

This brand she quenched in a cool well by,
Which from Love's fire took heart perpetual,
Growing a bath and healthy remedy
For men diseased; but I, my mistress' thrall.
Came there for cure and this by that I prove:
Love's fire heats water, water cools not love.

4:40:44

this morning.

So …you…thank you

What about

People

You

You

You

Get out of here

Sure

4:45:01

only 40 minutes to dawn

but….

If you change the value of the resident capacitor you change the frequency

That fine

Congratulations.

Dave was here at 3:00

It’s very demanding…..

Solved that problem…everyone that goes past the pitch goes up…it’s nearly over….really

Yea…oh really…need to go find a cigarette…go

4:57:36

are you going?

Yes

I couldn’t hear anything…

I could actually hear….

5:00:21

do you want some chocolate

to keep going…

it was fun

(yawn)

5:06:41

If you want to go

Back to your place

5:15:58

do you want to play

5:17:22

start cleaning up

5:18:21

Oh!

the right time

the right moment

5:20--

SHH!

Cage Musicircus, MIAF 2007

Holly Crawford is an artist, writer and curator.
She is the Director and founder of AC Institute an experimental spaces for research and exhibition in contemporary art (**www.artcurrents.org**) and publication of books on contemporary art and criticism. She taught art and art issue in the UCLA Art Department and at SVA. She received her Ph.D. from the University of Essex in Art History and Theory, B.A and M.A. in Economics and M.S. in Behavioral Science from UCLA. From 2004-2006, she was a non-clinical Fellow at NYU Medical School Psychoanalytic Center. She was born in California and now lives in New York City. Member AICA, CAA, & Art Table

Publications:
Outsourced Critics, Holly Crawford, project by & editor, essays by Jill Connor and Stephen Squibb,
AC Institute, 2010; "Who Gets to Play?' in Popular Culture Values and the Arts Essays on Elitism versus Democratization: edited by Ray B. Browne and Lawrence A. Kreiser, McFarland, 2009; Catalogue essay "Disney and Pop Art",for the catalogue Once Upon a Time Disney, Grand Palais and Fine Art Museum, Montreal, 2008; *Artistic Bedfellows* (editor), UPA/Roman & Littlefield, 2008; "Temporary Bedfellows: Claes Oldenburg, Maurice Tuchman and Disney," essay in *Artistic Bedfellows,* 2008; "Having Their Cake and Eating It Too: The case of Christo's and Jeanne-Claude's Im(permanence) and Exclusivity," essay in *Artistic Bedfellows*, 2008 (conference paper Carnegie Mellon); "Disney and Pop Art", *Once Upon a Time Disney*, Bruno Girveau, (Editor & Curator) Grand Palais and Fine Art Museum, Montreal (two editions-one in French and one in English) Prestel, 2007; *Attached to the Mouse, Disney and Contemporary Art* (2006) UPA/Roman & Littlefield, 2006; "What's New," catalogue essay, DIVA (Digital and Video Art Fair), Paris, 2005.

Contemporary Art Issues Video: *Critical Conversations in a Limo*, NY 2006 (In conjunction with the Armory as VIP project), 2007 in Melbourne (MIAF) & San Francisco (The LAB & Sesnon Gallery UCSC). 8 videos (18+ hours) of discussions about contemporary art

Selected Art Projects:
Her art and poetry (**www.art-poetry.info**) give new meanings and draws categories themselves into question through transformative juxtapositions. Many projects are ongoing, site specific and participatory. Selected projects: *Offerings* (Ars Electronica, (.net Participant, 1998); *May I have your autograph*? (unofficial, Basel Miami Art Fair 2007), *Critical Conversations in a Limo*, NY 2006 (VIP project, Armory), 2007 in Melbourne (MIAF) & San Francisco (The LAB & Sesnon Gallery UCSC). *Economic Crisis Observatory*, (Beacon Arts Building, LA,2012), *Orphans Offered Up* (2010 NYC, Lakeside Art Gallery University of Essex and Liverpool 2011); *Open Adoption* (Pool Art Fair 2005*),* Hospitality Suite (Pool Art Fair 2005), Hospitality Suite, DiVA, Paris, 2005, *Hyphens (*Gallery 303 NY Photography Fair & Brown Bag Contemporary San Francisco Photograph Fair*), Voice Over NYC to Wels (via Twitters) 2009,* MKH, Wels, Austria, *Found Punctuation (video)* Tate Modern 2007; *13 Ways of Looking at a Blackbird,* Riverside Art Museum & Florence, Valencia, London, NYC (The Lab) and Berlin; *The Road* and *Water, Water , Water,* Downey Art Museum.

Curated projects: *Sound Art Limo,* NY and Melbourne 2007, *Flatland Limo*, NYC 2008, and *Live in the Limo* was co-curated with Sonya Hofer, NYC 2009. Curated projects at AC Institute 2008-prsent. Co-curated with Sonja Hofer 2007-2008; with Sonja Hofer, Joseph DiPonio 2009-2010; with Joseph DiPonio and Nicole Bebout 2011-2012; Nicole Bebout 2012-2013.

Member: ACIA, CAA and Art Table.

www.ingramcontent.com/pod-product-compliance
Lightning Source LLC
LaVergne TN
LVHW081325110826
845149LV00007B/1600
* 9 7 8 0 9 8 5 2 4 6 1 2 9 *